Bev Spencer

YOU CAN'T DO THAT in CANADA!

Illustrations by **Steve Attoe**

Scholastic Canada Ltd.

To Beverley Marshall,
who knows how to be a friend

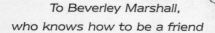

Scholastic Canada Ltd.
175 Hillmount Road, Markham, Ontario, Canada L6C 1Z7

Scholastic Inc.
555 Broadway, New York, NY 10012, USA

Scholastic Australia Pty Limited
PO Box 579, Gosford, NSW 2250, Australia

Scholastic New Zealand Limited
Private Bag 94407, Greenmount, Auckland, New Zealand

Scholastic Ltd.
Villiers House, Clarendon Avenue, Leamington Spa,
Warwickshire CV32 5PR, UK

Canadian Cataloguing in Publication Data

Spencer, Beverley
 You can't do that in Canada!

ISBN 0-590-51923-9
1. Law — Canada — Humor. 2. Law — Canada — Popular works. I. Title.
K184.7.C2S63 2000   349.71'0207   C99-932320-2

5 4 3   Printed and bound in Canada   1 2 3 4 /0

INTRODUCTION

About four thousand years ago the first written laws we know of were made. Shortly after that, someone probably said one of them was silly. We've been arguing ever since.

Canada's laws didn't start out trying to be odd or silly. There are thousands of rules made to help us live together peacefully. Some of them remind us to respect each other's privacy (no spying allowed in parks) or our right to get a good night's rest (no dog barking allowed at night). Some of them prevent chaos on the road. Can you imagine what it would be like if everyone drove on the side of the road they liked, instead of always the right-hand side? Every rule has been passed by vote in one of our governments. No matter how wacky they seem, there was once a good reason for making every law. Or at least, we think so!

Every level of government gets to make rules — federal and provincial, plus all cities, towns and townships. Bylaws are the rules made by towns or cities.

Some of the wacky laws and bylaws in this book might have changed by the time you read them. At this very moment someone is probably changing one, and repealing (or making invalid) another. And someone is writing a new law. The urge to make rules is endless. But a lot of old rules are gathering dust on a shelf somewhere, ignored. No one bothers to enforce them anymore, and it's too much trouble to change them — until one day someone objects, and an old bylaw is dusted off. Then the arguing really begins.

See if you can imagine what was behind the laws in this book.

FUR & FEATHERS, PAWS & LAWS

ACCORDING

to a judgment in Winnipeg in 1996, you can sit on an alligator, you can poke it and you can pull its tail — but none of this qualifies as illegally provoking or agitating it. Good thing, because in Winnipeg you can't provoke an alligator into a fight.

IN TORONTO

it is illegal to allow your pigeons to stray, perch, roost or rest upon anything not owned by you. Try telling that to a bird in flight!

AN OLD BYLAW in the City of Toronto reportedly made it illegal to drag a dead horse down Yonge Street on a Sunday.

YOU CAN'T HUNT big game in your comfortable blue sweats in Saskatchewan. All your outer clothing has to be blindingly bright scarlet, yellow, orange or white, or a combo. And if you want to stay within the legal requirements, a brightly coloured hat is a must. Pay attention to what day it is, too. All hunting of wildlife is prohibited on Sundays.

IT USED TO BE a crime to hunt in Quebec in a disguise.

PUBLIC SHOWS
where animals perform tricks to entertain people
are illegal in Oak Bay (a district in Victoria, B.C.)
unless the animals are horses, dogs or ponies.
This means that bears in tutus riding bicycles,
or tigers in cages, are not allowed.
Animals cannot be exploited for profit.

UNCONTROLLED animals are not allowed on highways in the Yukon. Allow your pet within 30 metres of the centre of the highway, out of your control, and the fine is $100. Do it three times within three years, and the fine is $500, and the government can take away your pet. This is serious pet and driver protection.

THERE used to be a reward of $20 for catching or helping catch a horse thief in the County of York, Ontario, but only if the thief was found guilty.

DON'T let your pet rat escape in Oak Bay, B.C. It's illegal to let rodents "run at large."

DO YOU exercise in a way that might frighten a horse? Then you can't do it in Quesnel, B.C., without permission.

A BRITISH COLUMBIA bylaw includes pit bull terriers in the definition of a vicious dog, no matter what the temper of the individual dog. One pit bull owner challenged the bylaw, saying it was an unlawful libel — giving his dog a "bad name." The court decided that the bylaw was "uncharitable," but that dogs weren't hurt by bad names.

IT IS an offence to tease or annoy any animals in Inuvik, Northwest Territories.

YOU MAY NOT establish a pigsty within 50 feet (about 15 metres) of a public place in Halifax County, Nova Scotia.

IN 1902 the Yukon prohibited the driving of dogs through the streets of any town or village faster than 6 miles an hour (almost 10 kilometres an hour). Possible fines were up to $50 plus costs.

In Inuvik, Northwest Territories, dogs must be "properly secured" and may not be tied to trees or shrubs.

VIETNAMESE potbellied pig Violet was given seven days to get out of town in 1994. Violet's two owners, who kept her at their pet store in Burlington, Ontario, were fined $1,400 each for keeping an exotic animal in the city.

THE FORMER City of Scarborough, Ontario, allowed residents to keep horses, ponies, donkeys or mules, but not if they had "ferocious habits." Then they were illegal. No horses could be kept in the house, either.

AN OLD LAW in British Columbia reportedly made it illegal to kill a sasquatch.

YOU AREN'T ALLOWED to keep a cow in your house in St. John's, Newfoundland. If you've got cows, and you want to get rid of them before the police catch you, better get up early. It's illegal to drive cattle through the streets of St. John's after 8 a.m.

NO PIGS were allowed to run at large in the streets of Toronto, as of 1834.

DOG OWNERS in Charlottetown, P.E.I., are guilty of an offense if their dogs disturb people by barking between 9:00 p.m. and 7:00 a.m. Shhh, pooch!

KEEPING two cows for more than two hours within 100 feet (about 30 metres) of an occupied building was prohibited in Calgary — unless you had written permission from the people in the building.

DON'T let your parrot squawk or talk too loudly in Oak Bay, B.C. If it disturbs someone, you'll get blamed, to the tune of $100.

PET TARANTULAS

are not allowed in Toronto. Spider lovers there
will have to choose a non-poisonous pet.
In parts of Canada where tarantulas are legal
as pets, watch out for the GST.
Pet stores will supply cockroaches to feed
your pet, but you have to pay about
four cents tax on each one.

YOU CAN'T own a pet bat in Toronto. Same thing goes for skunks — even friendly, unsmelly ones. No pet porcupines are allowed, either.

You may not own a snake which is poisonous, or one which (as an adult) will be longer than 3 metres, either. Lizards which will reach an adult length larger than 2 metres are forbidden, too.

IT IS AGAINST THE LAW in Nova Scotia to display, sell or give an artificially coloured chick, under the Baby Chick Protection Act.

Colour a baby chicken and you could go to jail for up to 30 days, or pay up to a $100 fine. Even if you give one to a friend, you are breaking the law.

IT IS AGAINST THE LAW to bring more than two birds of the parrot family into Canada from the United States at the same time. Then, you or members of your family can't bring more of these birds into Canada until 90 days have passed. And the birds must have been in your personal possession for 90 days before you bring them, and have had no contact with other birds. Whew!

YOU CAN'T keep more than two dogs over the age of four months in Oak Bay, B.C. If your pet dog has puppies, you have to write to the Licence Inspector to report the event within a month. It's a legal requirement.

Cat owners in Oak Bay have it a little easier. They are allowed to keep five cats per "parcel of land."

YOU CAN'T KEEP

a pet hare in Toronto,
but you can keep up to six pet rabbits.
If one of them has babies, though, they're illegal.
You already have your allowed number.

YOU'RE violating a bylaw if you own a snake greater than 2 feet (60 centimetres) in length in Dartmouth, Nova Scotia.

FIND a resting place for your dead goldfish, or flush it, if you live in Kanata, Ontario. It is illegal to deposit the carcass of any dead animal, fish or fowl on a street there.

IT IS ILLEGAL to leave your horse in front of the Country Squire hotel in Fort Qu'Appelle, Saskatchewan, without hitching it securely to the hitching post. However, the hitching post was removed many years ago . . . Same thing in East Toronto parks. You can't hitch your horse to anything but a hitching post, but — you guessed it — hitching posts are entirely missing from most parks.

ALLIGATORS and crocodiles
of any size whatsoever
are not allowed in private
Toronto homes.

IN COQUITLAM, B.C., cats over six months of age have to be spayed or neutered, unless a breeding permit is purchased. No unauthorized kittens are to be produced.

This is a big change. In the past, pro-cat laws inherited by Canada from Britain have given cats a lot more freedom than other pets such as dogs. In Britain, cats have been highly valued for centuries because of their skill in catching mice and rats.

YOU MAY NOT ride a horse, cow, sheep or other animal on any sidewalk in the Halifax Regional Municipality, Nova Scotia.

BIRD FEEDERS have been forbidden, at times, in Brossard, Pierrefonds and Côte St.-Luc, Quebec.

IT IS ILLEGAL to wear a snake in public in Fredericton, New Brunswick, or to carry your pet lizard on your shoulder. This bylaw was first created because one young man carried his pet boa constrictor downtown and into some stores. It caused a stir. So now "no person shall have, keep or possess a snake or other reptile upon the street or in any public place . . . [unless] it is in a case, cage or other container" that will completely confine the creature.

19

DEFINITELY

DIRTY

DEEDS

BARBED WIRE fences along or near any street in Calgary were forbidden in 1911. The penalty for having a barbed wire fence was $5 a day. (Why would anyone want a fence like that? In 1905 the city pound held more chickens and hogs than dogs, and the fences used then were to keep the animals from straying.)

UNTIL 1996 it was illegal for children to be out-of-doors alone in the evening in Edmonton. Children under the age of 14 (or children that looked that age) had to be indoors by nine o'clock from May to October, and by eight o'clock from November to April, "except for proper control or guardianship."

How did they know when the curfew had begun? Easy. "The town inquirer shall regularly ring the 'Curfew Bell' as a warning." Parents who didn't know where their children were after curfew could be fined $1 for the first offense, $2 for the second and $5 for the third. Parents who would not pay, and let their children "run wild," could be put in jail for up to 30 days. The curfew statute was passed in 1897, but it lived on (though unenforced) until the 1990s.

IT WAS AGAINST THE LAW to park a wagon, carriage or car closer to a house than 10 feet (about 3 metres) in Calgary.

IN CALGARY, from 1885 to 1996, people using the sidewalks or streets had to avoid running, racing, crowding or jostling each other. The throwing of snowballs, ice or stones was out, too.

No "charivaries" either. That was when someone banged kettles, pans and tea trays together under a chosen person's window. The penalties? A $50 fine or three weeks in jail!

IT'S A CRIME anywhere in Canada to be in an "unlawful assembly" or "riot." A huge, super-wild party might qualify. It's hard to believe, but if the police actually READ the Riot Act, and the noisy gathering does not break up right away, the penalty could be as much as life imprisonment.

IT USED TO BE ILLEGAL to skate or to go swimming or bowling before 1:30 p.m. or after 6:30 p.m. on Sundays in the former township of East York, Ontario. The sports had to be "conducted in an orderly and seemly manner." Movies could not be shown Sunday mornings, either.

It was illegal even to be present at a baseball game where a prize was at stake on Sunday mornings or evenings, after 1967.

These bylaws were passed in the 1960s. In 1986 the Lord's Day Act of Ontario was repealed, as a "violation of the guarantee to freedom of conscience and religion," but it took some municipalities a few years to bring their bylaws in line with the provincial law.

BE ON YOUR BEST

behaviour if the Queen visits. Doing anything intended to "alarm Her Majesty" is against the law. An adult who alarms her on purpose can spend up to 14 years in prison.

MORAL CONDUCT was dictated by

bylaws in the late 1800s, and some of it still is. For example, a bylaw passed in 1864 made it an offence to "utter any profane oath, or obscene, blasphemous or grossly insulting language, or to commit any other immorality or indecency in any street, highway, or other public places" in York and Peel Counties. It's still an offence to swear or insult someone in any of Ontario's provincial parks.

IN KANATA, Ontario, it is illegal to spit. Baseball players can't throw spitballs, either.

It's an offence to spit on a bus or in a subway station in Toronto.

It was made illegal to spit on Calgary sidewalks in 1907.

A 1910 bylaw in Saskatoon prohibits spitting on sidewalks, stairways, streetcars or in concert halls, churches, theatres or steam-boat waiting rooms, "except into a proper receptacle." As long as you hit the spittoon, you could even spit in church!

NO ONE CAN legally set off fireworks in Charlottetown, P.E.I., unless authorized by the Council. Firecrackers were illegal at all times in all parts of Scarborough, Ontario.

A 1911 CALGARY bylaw made it illegal to throw tacks, nails, barbed wire, glass or china on sidewalks, streets, lanes or alleyways, where a horse could be injured or a bicycle damaged.

A PERSON could be rewarded for reporting crimes against the public morals in the 1800s in Ontario's York and Peel Counties. When people broke the laws of "public morals" they were fined from $1 to $40. If they couldn't pay, anything they owned could be sold to pay the fine. If the offender didn't own enough, he could be sent to jail for up to 20 days, with or without hard labour. That was up to the judge. Moral conduct was a serious matter.

And the reward for reporting the crime? The informer got half the money.

BEFORE 1843, a person could be imprisoned for debts of less than £10 (serious money, in those days) in Upper Canada. After 1843, imprisonment for debts alone was abolished.

DUELLING IS A CRIME

anywhere in Canada. You may not "provoke
another person to fight a duel,"
or accept the challenge. You could face up to
two years in jail.
(The musketeers would have to put down their
swords and pistols if they lived here.)

IN CHARLOTTETOWN, P.E.I., a person has broken the "nuisance bylaw" if he "willfully or wantonly rings any doorbell or knocks at any door, building or fence so as to disturb or annoy any person in his dwelling, place of business, or meeting place." How do they sell Girl Guide cookies there?

Scarborough had a similar 1976 bylaw that made it an offence to "ring, blow horns, shout or cause or permit unusual noises or noises likely to disturb the inhabitants." The problem was, "unusual noises" weren't spelled out. Make them, though, and you were in violation of the bylaw.

IN MONTREAL it is illegal to wash your car in the street.

REPORTEDLY, no one may legally show affection in public on a Sunday in Wawa, Ontario.

IT IS ILLEGAL to spy on anyone in a Toronto park. It is an offence to spy on people in a city park in the Halifax Regional Municipality, too.

BEGGING FOR MONEY used to be an offence in Calgary. Beggars were also not permitted to expose diseased or malformed parts of their bodies in an attempt to get sympathy.

You're still committing a violation in Chicoutimi, Quebec, if you expose to public view a wound, ulcer or anything else hideous or monstrous.

A JUDGE in Collingwood, Ontario, decided it was an offence to let the Canadian flag "snap" too loudly in the wind. In February, 1999, he sent a summons for this crime to a retired schoolteacher.

NO ONE is allowed to make "noises or sounds that disturb or tend to disturb the quiet, peace, rest, enjoyment or comfort of the neighborhood" in Ottawa, without city council approval. Limits put on many sounds are between 48 and 55 decibels. By the way, bird song is between 50 and 60 decibels, so if you own a bird its singing could be illegal!

The anti-noise bylaw in Ottawa actually makes the buzzing of bees a violation. (No one knows how to enforce this one.)

How many decibels are involved in singing "Happy Birthday"? Strictly speaking, it's probably illegal too, unless you sing very softly.

In practice, someone has to complain before the police take action. If you live in Ottawa, invite all your neighbours to your party, to be safe.

NEED TO GET someone's attention? It was forbidden for the public to ring bells, use megaphones, blow horns, or use rattles in any street of Montreal for this purpose, without the written permission of the chief of police, according to an 1877 bylaw.

In 1885 it became illegal to advertise the sale of anything in Calgary by "the blowing of any horn, crying, hallowing, or creating any other discordant noise in any of the streets."

IT USED TO BE ILLEGAL to annoy your neighbours by insulting them in Edmonton. "No person shall make use of any profane, swearing, obscene, blasphemous, or grossly insulting language within the City of Edmonton which is likely to cause a breach of the peace or . . . to cause annoyance to any person or persons in the neighbourhood."

THERE IS STILL

a Halloween curfew in Charlottetown, P.E.I. Young people under 16 may not be in a public place after 8:00 p.m. on Halloween night, unless accompanied by someone over the age of 18. Fines for breaking curfew are from $100 to $500, or up to 90 days in jail.

INDECENT EXPOSURE is still

an offence in most places in Canada, but the definitions of a sufficient bathing dress have changed a lot:

It is now legal for women to go topless on Ontario streets. Bathing doesn't even come into it.

But in the early 1970s it was unlawful to wear a partially transparent bathing suit in Victoria, B.C.

IT WAS LEGAL to sunbathe in your "birthday suit" at Toronto's Hanlan's Point Beach in 1999, but not to go in the water. Legally, swimsuits were still required when you swam, according to a 65-year-old bylaw, even though the beach had been opened as "clothing optional" in May of 1999. Police chased bathers out of the water one day, and gave out tickets and cautions. Everyone laughed, because people had been skinny-dipping and sunbathing there for decades. A bylaw was later passed making skinny-dipping legal.

IT WAS A VIOLATION to bathe near any public highway between 7:00 a.m. and 8:00 p.m., without wearing "a proper bathing dress sufficient to prevent any indecent exposure of the person" in Ontario's York and Peel Counties, as of 1864.

IT IS AN offence to put out your garbage in small, thin bags in St. John's, Newfoundland. The bags have to be at least 1.5 millimetres in thickness, with no smaller than a 25-litre capacity, and no bigger than a 90-litre capacity, measuring at the smallest 66 by 91 centimetres in size. Whew — and not just because of the smell!

GARBAGE in Oak Bay, B.C., can't ooze. It's illegal to put any damp or wet substance into a garbage can or bag, unless it has been drained, wrapped and sealed in watertight plastic bags or material, "so as not to ooze or leak." Garbage crews can refuse to empty any garbage can filled beyond 2 centimetres from the top, too. And finally, garbage cans have to be kept clean. If they're not, they don't meet regulations, and crews don't have to touch them.

SWIMMING in the Don River in East York, Ontario, (between 1931 to 1996) could cost offenders a $50 fine, or up to 21 days in jail.

NO ONE was allowed to ride a mini-bike along sidewalks or pathways intended for pedestrians, on any highway or bridge in Scarborough, Ontario, in the 1970s. The fine could be as high as $300.

IT IS AN OFFENCE to let the fish you caught in national park waters go rotten, if it was fit to be eaten.

OUTDOORS OUTLAWS

YOU MAY NOT leave
a fishing line unattended in a
national park, when fishing with
a rod or hand-held line.

IT IS ILLEGAL to buy or sell fish caught
under a domestic fishing licence in Alberta.
A person can have the fish if "the resident is
in dire need of fish for the purpose of feeding
his family or animals he owns." If a restaurant
needs fish for its menu, that doesn't qualify
— the fish caught can't be sold to an eatery.

BICYCLISTS in Scarborough were
committing an offence if they carried any
package which prevented the rider from
keeping both hands on the handlebars.

IN SOME PARTS
of Kanata, Ontario,
you cannot keep a boat or a trailer in sight of
the neighbours . . . not even on your own driveway.

CYCLISTS in Vancouver must paint
22.5 centimetres of their rear fenders white.
(That gets tricky for some cyclists, because
rear fenders are not required in Vancouver.)

IN OTTAWA, you are not legally allowed
to remove your feet from the pedals while
cycling, when the bicycle is in motion.
   This is hard to do after you've come to a
stop and you're getting back into motion.

YOU MAY NOT CUT DOWN
more than one tree a year that's over 8 inches
(20 centimetres) in width in your own yard,
without a permit, in Vancouver. Sizable
trees in Toronto get similar protection.
And in Winnipeg, if a tree is larger than
10 centimetres in diameter, it cannot be
transplanted. But Charlottetown, P.E.I., takes
the tree-hugger prize — there it's a violation
to injure any tree.

YOU MAY NOT use a siren on your bicycle in a national park, but a bell, gong or horn can be used. In fact, it MUST be sounded before passing a vehicle or person travelling in the same direction as your bicycle.

A BICYCLIST who gives an incorrect name and address, when asked by a police officer who spots him or her breaking a law or bylaw, can be arrested on the spot in Ontario.

IN ALBERTA you may not hunt wildlife using a flashlight.

STRANGE CRIMES

IF A NEWSPAPER

reports as true something it knows is not true, that's called "spreading false news," a crime punishable by up to two years in jail.

IT'S ILLEGAL

to name a store or anything for sale "Parliament Hill." That name is reserved for the part of Ottawa where the parliament buildings are located. This crime carries a pretty stiff fine — up to $2,000, or up to six months in jail.

IT'S A CRIME to stop a member of the clergy from "performing any . . . function in connection with his calling."

IT'S A CRIME TO PRETEND to practise witchcraft in Canada. The penalty is up to two years in prison.

Telling fortunes and reading tea leaves for money are crimes, too. According to Section 365 of the Criminal Code, "Everyone who fraudulently . . . pretends to exercise or to use any kind of witchcraft, sorcery, enchantment or conjuration [or] undertakes for a consideration to tell fortunes, or . . . pretends from his skill or knowledge of an occult or crafty science to discover where or in what manner anything that is stolen or lost may be found . . . is guilty." In 1984 a woman in Quebec was charged under this law. The case relied on whether she believed her own predictions were true.

Tea leaf readers in Toronto avoid being prosecuted under this law by charging for the cup of tea. The reading is free.

PALM READERS in Edmonton had to give the Licence Inspector proof of their ability to "carry on the calling," after 1917. At least two "well-known and reputable ratepayers" had to vouch for the palm readers' "good moral character." And they had to be able to read and write either English or French. "No licence [was] granted to an alien enemy." (Alien enemy? No, not someone from outer space. The law probably referred to anyone born outside Canada and considered an enemy of Canada during World War I.)

IT'S A VIOLATION to offer a reward for the return of anything lost or stolen and promise that no questions will be asked. It's even illegal to print or publish the offer. (Questions will be asked, and you could be answering them.)

THE CRIMINAL CODE allows a two-year penalty for "offending a public place with a bad smell."

KNOWINGLY

selling anything "defective" to the
Queen or her agents is a criminal act.
Do it and you could face up to
14 years in jail!

47

DISTURBING

an oyster bed
is a crime
anywhere in Canada.

SINCE APRIL FOOL'S DAY,

1999, it is illegal to go canoeing, kayaking or rowing anywhere in Canada without a flashlight and a whistle. You'll need 15 metres of "buoyant heaving line," a bailing bucket and an anchor, too. The anchor has to have at least 15 metres of cable, rope or chain attached to it. But have no fear — if you don't have an anchor, you can still avoid unlawful behaviour. You'll just have to leave the "manual propelling devices" at home. In other words, go rowing without the paddles, and you don't need an anchor. (Hmmm, if you could go rowing without the paddles, you probably wouldn't need the boat, either.)

UNTIL 1997 no one was allowed to grow wildflowers in a natural setting in the City of Toronto. (In bygone times certain wildflowers could invade and ruin a farmer's crop.)

In more recent times neighbours objected to having a yard full of wildflowers next door. In 1993 an environmentalist was charged with growing wildflowers in her yard, and fined. It took four years for the appeal, and finally the amendment to the bylaw. Now "natural gardens" are legal in Toronto, but uncut, long grass on lawns is still illegal.

In Halifax, they even measure it: People may not allow the grass between the curb and the sidewalk to grow to more than 6 inches (15 centimetres) in height.

IN THE HALIFAX
Regional Municipality, no one can remove bark
from a tree without permission.

PROPERTY DOS AND DON'TS

IN QUESNEL, B.C., it is still a legal requirement to have an outside privy, at least 20 feet (6 metres) from your house, but not more than 100 feet (30 metres). The privy has to be "fly tight," too.

Do they have indoor plumbing in Quesnel? They do. But the privy bylaw still stands.

SMALL toilet rooms
are illegal in Halifax.
It's a violation to have a toilet room less
than 10 feet (about 1 metre) square.

SINGING in the privy used to be forbidden in Manitoba, if the privy was attached to a restaurant or tavern where wine could be served.

IN WOLFVILLE, Nova Scotia, "no person shall wantonly unhinge, take away or hide" any front gate.

A LITTLE GIRL'S outdoor playhouse was ruled unlawful in Kanata, Ontario, a few years ago, because it was taller than the accepted height for garden sheds.

IN THOMPSON, Manitoba, it is illegal to live in a truck, bus, railcar or streetcar.

DURING THE 1800s in Toronto, chimneys had to be swept once every six weeks in winter and spring.

THE SIZE OF SNOWMEN

on a corner lot in Souris, P.E.I., used to be limited to no more than 30 inches (76 centimetres).

BEING NAKED inside your own house used to be illegal in Winnipeg unless your blinds were drawn.

ACCORDING to the Alberta legislature, it is illegal to paint a wooden ladder in that province.

OTHER WEIRD & WACKY LAWS

PRETENDING to be drunk in St. Stephen, New Brunswick, used to be an offence.

A TEENAGER can't legally walk down the main street in Fort Qu'Appelle, Saskatchewan, with his shoes untied.

UNTIL 1994 girls and women who wore shorts in public in Hull, Quebec, were committing a violation.

SOME TORONTO SCHOOLS

have odd clothing laws. If students at Branksome Hall wear any shoes other than flat black oxfords, or flat black penny loafers without decorations, the shoes must be left in the general office, and the student must wear office-issued black slippers for the day. The offending shoes can be reclaimed at the end of the school day.

Kilts and tunics at Havergal College are to be worn exactly 7.5 centimetres above the knee. At Bayview Glen School boys may not wear earrings, and girls' earrings can only be small gold, silver or pearl studs.

IT IS ILLEGAL

to paint a bus bright yellow in Ontario, unless it is used to carry school or preschool children, or handicapped adults.

No public vehicle or school bus in Ontario is allowed to change gears while crossing a railway track, either.

IT WAS AN OFFENCE to wear
a bathing suit in the park in Outremont,
Quebec, during the early 1990s.

In Toronto, a bylaw banned sunbathing in
High Park. In 1994 a man was fined for
refusing to put on his shirt. His case became
famous and the bylaw was later changed.

DO YOUR PARENTS have an
in-home business in Swift Current,
Saskatchewan? Then forget about starting
your own lemonade stand or other business.
Only one business per home is allowed there,
and friends can't volunteer to help you, either.
They would be violating a bylaw if they did.

IT IS ILLEGAL for elementary school
children in New Brunswick to sell chocolate
bars door-to-door in order to raise money for
their schools.

TAXI DRIVERS

in the Halifax Regional Municipality
must wear socks.

A BYLAW

in Chicoutimi, Quebec,
forbids being masked or in disguise
in public.

LEGALLY, every case of the flu in St. John's, Newfoundland, had to be reported to the City Medical Officer within 24 hours, from 1937 to 1995. If a doctor had reason to believe that anyone within the city limits had an infectious disease, including the flu, he or she had to "give notice." The penalty for not doing so was between $10 and $50.

IN DORVAL, Quebec, visitors from out of town must pay for the visit of a firetruck — even if they didn't need it, and didn't call the fire department. In 1994 a woman extinguished a small fire under the hood of her car, and then discovered a passerby on the road had called the fire department. The fire was out when the firetruck arrived. The bill came to $495.

FIRECRACKERS may not be exploded in Oak Bay, B.C.

It's illegal to sell a roman candle there except as part of a "family pack," and fireworks displays are not allowed in any park or street.

FOR A SHORT TIME in 1999 in Nunavut, the Fire Department bylaw stated that "any applicant to the fire department must have a history of mental illness." (Of course, it should have said: "any applicant to the fire department must NOT have a history of mental illness.") The typo got passed by council by accident, but was soon spotted by an eagle-eyed reader. A rewritten version was drafted shortly thereafter.

IN 1868 it became illegal to play games in a cemetery in Toronto. The penalty was a fine of $50.

IT USED to be illegal for men to refuse to work, without pay, on local highways, as "statutory labor," a standard part of life in most places in Canada in the late 1800s.

The Nova Scotia statutes of 1873 outlined it: "Every male between the ages of sixteen and sixty, being able to do a reasonable day's work, shall be liable to perform two days' labor as a poll tax," on six days notice. The men were expected to bring their own tools. If a man owned property, more work was required. If a property was assessed as being worth $4,000, 12 days of labor were added to the poll tax. A man could pay the roads commissioners instead of working, at 50 cents per day. If he didn't pay in advance, the cost went up to 60 cents a day.

IN QUEBEC, English signs must be no more than one-third the size of their French counterparts. This law was created to help protect the French language.

A customer in Napierville may have gone too far when she said a shop was breaking the law because it showed her a parrot that could speak only English.

BONGO DRUMMING is forbidden in downtown Victoria, B.C.

IN QUEBEC, the government can object to a baby's legal name — both first and last names. Parents can go to court if they wish to keep the names they have chosen for their child, but they can still be refused. In 1998 the government objected to the middle name, "c'est-un-ange," meaning "it's an angel."

IT'S AN OFFENCE for a commercial AM or FM radio station to play only part of a Canadian song in their broadcasts. The whole song has to be played — no shortcuts allowed.

A CHIPPED or cracked bathtub is a violation in Dartmouth, Nova Scotia.

PEOPLE IN CALGARY didn't like to duck. It was illegal to put up an awning or sign less than 7 feet (about 2 metres) above the sidewalk.

BEGINNING IN 1834, it was illegal to get or give a smallpox inoculation in Toronto. The doctor was fined £5 (considerable money back then) for each shot.

IN LACHINE,

Quebec, a woman was sentenced
to 14 days in jail in 1993
for unpaid library fines.
She had refused to pay the fines
or to do community work.

IN 1912 it was illegal for moving picture machines to be driven by motors in Calgary. The machines had to be operated by hand.

IN ORDER to allow the study of anatomy, a Toronto bylaw in 1843 allowed unclaimed bodies, or the bodies of people supported by the province, to be delivered to medical schools or doctors having three or more pupils, for dissection . . . but not if the dying person objected. A doctor wanting a body had to appear before a judge and deposit £20, and £10 each for burial of the bodies after classes were over.

POWER SAWS cannot be operated outdoors on Sundays near a beach in Oak Bay, B.C. Operating them in the evenings in such places is forbidden, too. Stop your power saws at 7:00 p.m., or face a $50 fine.

IN BRITISH COLUMBIA

you can't have more than three televisions
in a restaurant, and they must be
small-screen televisions. In Vernon
a restaurant was allowed seven TVs,
but denied a pool table. In Campbell River
the same chain of restaurant put in eight TVs,
then was told to remove five.
Battles about the number and size of
televisions in restaurants have been fought,
by both letter and appeal.

WHY NOT IN THE PARK?

IT IS ILLEGAL to wade in Toronto park fountains, ponds, lakes or streams, unless the water is posted for bathing. So keep your little brother's toes out of the water!

SKATING or roller skating on any highway in a townsite or subdivision within a national park is forbidden.

WASTING game meat in Manitoba's Wood Buffalo National Park is unlawful. You can't abandon game meat, or feed it to dogs, if it is fit for human consumption.

IN KINGSTON, Ontario, no one was allowed to take worms from a park without written permission.

YOU MAY NOT pick up abandoned balls on the golf courses in Toronto parks. Even if there are a dozen lost balls in the bushes on one of these courses, with no owners in sight, "finders keepers" does not apply. Legally, you've got to leave those balls where they are.

AFTER 1902 it was forbidden to let your horse, cattle or swine eat the grass in a public park in Montreal. The animals could be taken away to the pound.

IN PARKS in Oak Bay, B.C., no one is allowed to damage a rock. (In Toronto parks it's a little different — no one is allowed to CLIMB rocks.)

MOVIE THEATRES in our national parks used to be awash with regulations. Until 1980:

A matron had to be on duty in the theatre if an unaccompanied person under 14 years of age attended a movie there. The matron had to be 18 years of age or older and dressed in a uniform approved by the superintendent of the park.

Children and young teens couldn't attend a movie after 8:00 p.m., even if the matron was present.

The national anthem had to be played at the end of each movie.

It was illegal to allow any film to travel through a projector at more than 100 feet (about 30 metres) per minute.

Local censors had to approve the movies.

It was an offence for the projection room to be dirty.

IT IS ILLEGAL

to release ten or more balloons inflated with
lighter-than-air gases within a twenty-four-hour period
in any City of Toronto park.

PEOPLE OVER 16 years of age were forbidden to use the playground equipment in Grande Prairie, Alberta.

THE OWNER of any animal that dies or has been killed on a national park highway must have the carcass removed "forthwith." However, it is illegal to haul any dead animal along a park highway during daylight without the permission of the park superintendent.

FROM 1902 to the early 1970s, it was illegal to take up more than one space on a Montreal park bench. Standing on a park bench was an offence, too, or sitting on the stone curbs in the parks.

IT USED TO BE AN OFFENCE to fasten a horse or other animal to a tree or shrub in Toronto. Nailing your hammock into a tree in a Toronto park is forbidden, too.

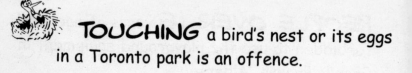 **TOUCHING** a bird's nest or its eggs in a Toronto park is an offence.

IN WINDSOR, Ontario, parks you are forbidden to play a flute, recorder or mouth organ, without a permit. In fact, it is illegal to play ANY instrument without a permit, except for unamplified stringed instruments, like guitars and violins.

HIGH PARK in Toronto used to have some mean tobogganing hills, even one named "Suicide Hill." No one could use them on Sundays, though. From 1912 on it was illegal to go tobogganing on park hill slides. Police were posted to make sure no one did it. Sunday tobogganing in Toronto parks didn't become legal until 1961. In the 1940s an American visitor called Toronto a "sanctimonious ice box," because of this kind of law against Sunday sports.

SHOPPING SHAKE-DOWNS

ANYWHERE IN Canada, you may not legally pay for a 26-cent item with 26 pennies. The limit is 25 cents. If you're paying in nickels, it's illegal to use more than $5 worth. You are not allowed to pay for something costing more than $10 entirely in dimes.

NO ONE under 16 years of age may work in bowling alleys or shooting galleries in Nova Scotia.

A LAW was passed in British Columbia making it illegal to squeeze or "manhandle" fruit at public vending stalls, unless you had already bought it.

A LOT OF ILLEGAL bread was baked and eaten in Edmonton until recently. It was a violation to sell unwrapped bread unless it weighed 24 ounces (680 grams), or wrapped bread unless it weighed 20 ounces (566 grams). This bylaw was in force from 1918 until 1996.

UNTIL 1996 it was illegal for bars to sell drinks during voting hours in an election, and for liquor stores to sell liquor.

IN THE 1970s it was illegal for ladies' hairdressers to give haircuts to boys eight years of age or older, in British Columbia.

IN 1997 the margarine police caught a grocery story in Alma, Quebec, with butter-coloured margarine in stock. It is illegal in Quebec for margarine to be the same colour as butter. The grocer had to remove the margarine from his shelves.

Quebec is the only place in North America, possibly the world, where this law still remains in force, but margarine has been banned before. In 1886 margarine of any colour was banned from the whole of Canada. It took a Privy Council decision to overturn that law in 1948.

The tempest in a tub continued to rage in Quebec. In 1953 the Quebec government even tried to introduce a law rewarding people for snitching on their neighbours. It was illegal to have margarine in your own home fridge!

It costs about $100,000 a month for Quebec to produce non-butter-coloured margarine. Butter-coloured imports are banned, too.

IT IS A VIOLATION to have an unlicensed going-out-of-business sale in Halifax.

IT'S A CRIME to burn money. That's called defacing "current coin" under Section 456 of Canada's Criminal Code.

In 1998 a man was fined in Sherbrooke, Quebec, for setting fire to a $20 bill.

IF ANY WEIGHT or measure in the early Toronto market was wrong, the goods for sale used to be taken away and given to the poor, and the merchant fined.

IT IS ILLEGAL for coffee shops and restaurants to set out tables and chairs from October 31 until April 1 in Edmonton, no matter how good the weather. Shop owners have broken this law when it was just too nice to sit inside.

IT IS ILLEGAL to make a sandwich or leave it in a room that contains a urinal, in Halifax. No food can be prepared or stored in such a room, even in a sealed container.

IN 1907 it was an offence for Edmonton barber shops to be open before five o'clock in the morning.

IF A BARBER worked in his shop after ten o'clock in the morning on a Sunday in Montreal, he could be fined or face up to two months in prison.

ON SUNDAYS during the 1800s all unnecessary work in Toronto was forbidden, and buying or selling anything was an offence, with one exception. Milk could be sold before nine o'clock in the morning, and after four o'clock in the afternoon.

SINS OF THE STREETS

IF YOU'RE under the age of 15, you may not legally be out on any street in Wolfville, Nova Scotia, after nine o'clock at night from October to March, and ten o'clock in the summer, without your parent or your guardian.

The curfew bylaw is still in force in Wolfville, though the chief of police there cannot remember it being enforced in the last 20 years.

IT'S AGAINST THE LAW to travel on an Ontario highway in a horse-drawn sleigh or sled without two bells attached to the harness or the sleigh. Travel with just one bell and you could be fined up to $5.

NO MATTER how good the ice on the streets or sidewalks of Kingston, Ontario, it's a violation to make a slide on it. Skating is out, too.

YOU CAN'T drop off a raccoon "out of its immediate area" after you've "live trapped" it, in Ontario. Get caught and you face a fine of up to $25,000.

IN THE 1970s cyclists were still required to have a kerosene lantern in plain view after dark, in Glace Bay, Nova Scotia.

CALGARY actually used to have a person called a Fence Viewer, who decided whether the fence to enclose animals or birds was "lawful or reasonable." The Fence Viewer could be fined for neglecting to do his duty when there was a dispute, and property had been damaged by animals.

IN MONTAGUE, P.E.I., it used to be forbidden to put any parts of buildings in the town dump. Restaurant owners couldn't put their potato or apple peelings there either.

Is it still forbidden? No. There is no dump in the town anymore.

IT'S ILLEGAL to cause "significant injury" to a tree's roots in Toronto, unless the owner consents. Neighbours can't put up a building too close to the tree next door, even when million-dollar investments are at stake.

IMMIGRANTS of French-speaking parents may not send their children to an English school in Quebec. Even immigrants from Britain or the United States can't do it. Their children must go to a school where all subjects are taught in French.

This is part of Bill 101, the language law, created to protect French culture in Quebec. There have been scores of fights over Bill 101. This one is going to be taken to the United Nations! Quebec's Equality Party filed a complaint in 1999 with the United Nations Educational, Scientific and Cultural Organization (UNESCO). UNESCO's charter says countries may have different school systems based on religion or language, but only if participation is optional.

NO SPLASHING in the water troughs on the streets of Edmonton was allowed after 1917. The water troughs were for the use of the travelling public and for watering animals only. Taking water away was forbidden, too.

NO ONE OVER the age of 10 may rollerblade on the sidewalks of local streets in Kingston, Ontario. (The streets are listed, in case of disagreement over which ones are local.)

SKATEBOARDING is illegal in the central business district of Swift Current, Saskatchewan. Do it, and a police officer can take your skateboard away from you and place it in the city compound. You'll have 30 days to reclaim the board there.

PEOPLE MAY NOT

dress as inanimate objects, stand on the sidewalk
and wave to people to advertise something,
in Victoria, B.C.
Luggie the Rug and his buddy (dressed as a cell
phone) were mascots in the 1990s, advertising rug
and phone services. They broke the bylaw,
and faced fines up to $100.

IT'S FORBIDDEN to bring a bicycle or an animal onto Toronto streetcars, buses or subways during morning and evening rush hours on weekdays, or at any other time that the vehicles are "heavily loaded."

You and your pet will have to wait, unless it's a seeing-eye or hearing-ear dog. If you squeeze on anyway, you may have to pay a fine of between $100 and $500.

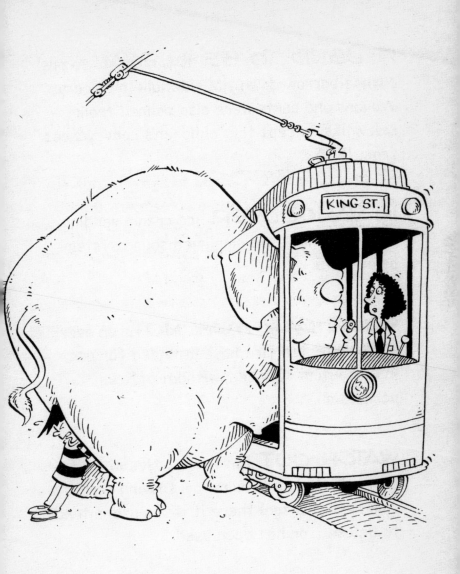

IT USED TO BE ILLEGAL to push a wheelbarrow down the sidewalk in Calgary. Wagons and carts were also banned from sidewalks, except for "children's conveyances," from 1885.

IN VANCOUVER, ice cream vending trucks cannot used amplified sound systems, as of 1995.

YOUR CAR MAY NOT run over an unprotected fire hose intended for use in Chicoutimi, Quebec, without official permission.

WATCH OUT for those hoses in Swift Current, Saskatchewan, too. Driving across a fire hose is illegal there if it's in use, intended to be used, or has been used.

CYCLING TRICKS are illegal in Swift Current, Saskatchewan. Bicycle riders must also keep at least one hand on the handlebars at all times. It is an offence to put a bicycle in a reclining position on any street, sidewalk or public place, too.

IN THE CITY OF HALIFAX it's an offence to perform ropewalking, gymnastics or athletic feats on a city sidewalk.

YOU COULD PAY a $75 fine if you bathe unlawfully on the property of the National Capital Commission.

IN HALIFAX COUNTY it is a violation to ring a doorbell, shout or knock on a door after 10 p.m.

IT USED TO BE ILLEGAL to leave a vehicle on the street in Calgary unless a horse was attached to it, according to an 1885 bylaw.

BILLY-GOATS could not be let loose on Edmonton streets.

CATTLE, SHEEP, PIGS or poultry could be driven through the streets of Edmonton, but bulls, stallions, boars, rams and he-goats had to be roped or bridled and held by someone.

IN DARTMOUTH, Nova Scotia, it may still be illegal to allow a chicken to cross a road.

ANNOYING OTHER passengers on streetcars in Edmonton used to be forbidden.

IT WAS ILLEGAL to go tobogganing on any street or highway in Ontario's York Township.

DON'T WALK on the lines on the streets in Prince Albert, Saskatchewan, if they've just been painted. It's illegal to "willfully drive or walk" on or over them. In Swift Current it's only illegal if the line is marked by a sign, flag or warning device.

IT WAS FORBIDDEN to auction horses, carriages or anything else on the sidewalks or streets of Toronto without permission from the Board of Works.

IT WAS A VIOLATION for any boy under the age of 10 or any girl under the age of 16 to sell newspapers on the streets of Edmonton, or to shine shoes, until 1992. The Public Convenience bylaw of 1947 made it illegal. (Who was the bylaw convenient for, then? Boys aged 10 to 16, supposedly, who got all the corner newspaper sales to themselves!)

IT USED TO BE an offence to let your gate swing open across any sidewalk in Calgary.

NEARLY all residents in Kanata, Ontario, will break the new Care of Streets bylaw when they shovel snow from sidewalks and driveways onto their roadside front lawns. That lawn area is city property, and snow may not be shovelled onto it.

IN ALBERT CAMPBELL Square, formerly part of the Scarborough Civic Centre in Ontario, it is forbidden to climb anything, to sit on plant containers, to throw coins or anything else into the pool, to play with a ball, to play any game such as baseball, cricket, croquet, football, golf, rugby, soccer or tennis, or to hold a horse race. Noisy demonstrations are not allowed, either.

IT WAS AN OFFENCE to drive horses without strong reins in Toronto, to gallop, or to drive at an "immoderate gait."

IT IS ILLEGAL to use profane language in a city park in Halifax, or to indulge in "boisterous behaviour."

YOU ARE BREAKING a bylaw if you skateboard on Fredericton, New Brunswick, streets.

HORSES COULD NOT stand on some Edmonton streets longer than 20 minutes. After 1920, people doing their business in a store had to get it done quickly, mount their horse or get in their carriage and be on their way.

SIDEWALK SALES used to be a violation in Toronto.

BUSKERS (street musicians) are not allowed to hand out balloon animals to children in Victoria, B.C.

YOU CAN GET A TICKET ON THE SPOT FOR COMMITTING ANY OF THESE INFRACTIONS:

FUN FINES

DON'T SWEAR

on Parliament Hill. You break a federal regulation if you use "blasphemous or indecent language" in the nation's capital, on federally owned land, and can be fined $100.

YOU MAY NOT

throw stones on the same government property, fire a BB gun or launch a missile in an "undesignated area" — that could get you fined $100.

YOU MAY NOT allow a llama to eat the grass in a national park. Letting a horse or mule graze there is illegal too. The fine is $74. But if you allow the same animals to eat the grass in a wildlife area in the same park, the fine goes up to $300. Why llamas? People are using llamas as pack animals on treks into the wilderness areas of our Canadian parks, because the llamas can carry more weight in camping gear than mules. But how do you stop a hungry llama from nibbling the greenery?

BLOCKING a waterway in a national park can get you fined $100. (Did anybody ever mention that to the beavers?)

IT IS ILLEGAL to smoke in a federal workplace. Smoke and you face a fine of $50.

But there's another catch: If your bosses "fail to ensure persons do not smoke" they face a fine of $500. It seems as if it's almost better to be the offender than the offender's employer — it costs less.

YOU MAY NOT display flags without written permission on Parliament Hill. Fly them anyway, and you could be fined $75.

IT IS FORBIDDEN to possess a slingshot in a wildlife area in national parks, even if you don't use it. Having it in your back pocket or pack can cost you $200.

YOU MAY BE FINED

$75 if your dog bites someone in a national park. Not only that, if your dog "molests wildlife" — bites an animal in a national park — you face the same fine. Time to get out the leash. And if you fail to stoop and scoop the doggy doo, a $50 fine applies.

IT IS AN INFRACTION to knowingly give a false answer to a question put by an enrolment officer of the National Defence. That lie could cost you $100.

IF YOU'RE a member of the National Defence reserve, you may not miss taking part in a scheduled parade. The penalty is $25 to $50.

INTERRUPTING the Canadian Forces while they're training, or hindering them while they're on the march, carries a $100 fine.

   Do you know someone who wants to join Canada's armed forces? Don't interfere. Impeding or interfering with the "recruiting of Canada forces" carries a hefty penalty — $300.

FIND A CRIPPLED or injured migratory game bird, and you must kill it immediately. Failing to do so can cost you $200 in fines in all national park wildlife areas.

ROAD RENEGADES

IT USED TO BE ILLEGAL

to drive on the right-hand side of the road in Victoria, B.C. Until 1921 everyone drove on the left side, as they do in Britain today. At midnight on the last day of 1921 all the drivers — including drivers of streetcars, and cyclists — changed sides.

YOU MAY NOT drive a horse or other animal, or a car or any other vehicle, through Bowring Park in St. John's, Newfoundland, at more than 10 miles (16 kilometres) per hour. No speeding in the park.

After ambling along on your horse in Bowring Park, be careful if you decide to dismount — you can't let go of your horse's bridle for any reason. To let go, you'd have to hitch the bridle to a hitching post (as is the case in many other parks). It's the only legal possibility. It's an offence to hitch the horse to any tree, fence, railing or other structure. The "hitch" is, though, there are no hitching posts anymore.

IT IS UNLAWFUL to drive a dog or dog team on a sidewalk of a settlement in the Northwest Territories.

IT IS ILLEGAL TO DRIVE so slowly on Ontario highways that you block the reasonable movement of traffic, unless safety requires it.

IT IS ILLEGAL to play hacky-sack in downtown Nelson, B.C. Also banned are unlicensed street music performers, drummers and dogs.

YOU'RE BREAKING a law if you put a SLOW-MOVING VEHICLE sign on a vehicle that isn't slow moving, on Ontario highways.

IT IS AGAINST THE LAW to drive an aircraft along a highway in Ontario, unless it complies with all the rules of the Highway Traffic Act.

IT IS ILLEGAL to drive a hovercraft on an Ontario highway. All air cushion vehicles are prohibited.

IN CHICOUTIMI, Quebec, it's an offence to play ball or hockey on any public road unless it is designated "rue de jeux" by the town council.

YOU'RE BREAKING THE LAW if you leave an aircraft on an Ontario highway after an emergency landing, longer than is absolutely necessary.

If the pilot in command is physically capable, he or she has to remove the aircraft or "cause it to be removed . . . as soon after landing as is reasonably possible." However, the pilot can't take off from the highway unless the police are present to provide traffic control, and another licensed commercial pilot, besides the owner, is satisfied that the plane is airworthy and the improvised runway is clear. Clearance from an air traffic controller is also required if weather conditions aren't right for visual flight rules.

Can't meet all these conditions? A fine of up to $10,000 applies.

STREET HOCKEY is a violation in Mount Royal and in Montreal, Quebec.

IT'S AN OFFENCE to play hockey in the streets of Nepean, Ontario, too.

YOU'D THINK PEOPLE WOULD KNOW BETTER

YOU'D THINK it wouldn't have to be spelled out, but drivers on Ontario highways can't watch television. Your motor vehicle can't be equipped with a television set in the front seat or on the dashboard on an Ontario highway. It's against the law to have a television screen visible to the driver while he or she is operating the vehicle.

ANYONE

who leaves an animal in distress
in the Yukon could face a fine of up to $500, or
up to six months in jail. The animal's owner must
"forthwith take appropriate steps to relieve its
distress," or face the consequences.

IT'S A BYLAW violation to throw hammers, bullets or other missiles in any public streets in Kingston. A bylaw prohibits the killing of any animal in a public street there, too.

ALLOW YOUR DOG to terrorize a person or animal in Oak Bay, B.C., and you could be paying a $200 fine.

IT'S NOT JUST dangerous to ride a bicycle at night in a national park without a headlamp and rear reflector. It's an offence.

A $500 FINE applies if you bring explosives onto St. Lawrence Seaway property without written permission.

IT'S A VIOLATION

to encourage dogs to fight
in any public street or place
in Kingston, Ontario.

THE UNLAWFUL QUIZ

Three of these laws are made up.
The rest are real.
Can you spot the fakes?
Check the back page for the answers.
Don't feel bad if you get them wrong —
who knew you couldn't do that in Canada?

1. It is an offence to sell artificial cheeses in Ontario.

2. Pet rats are not allowed in Toronto.

3. It's illegal to drive a toy car on a Toronto street.

4. Mobile home parks may not have a flashing entrance sign in Halifax County.

5. It used to be an offence to race across a bridge in Calgary. No one could cross faster than at a walk.

6. It was illegal to run a stable for horses in East York, Ontario, after 1912.

7. In Oshawa, Ontario, it used to be illegal to climb trees.

8. It is prohibited to let sheep stray in Point Pleasant Park, Halifax.

9. Rules applied to walking on Edmonton sidewalks as of 1915. People were not allowed to pass each other on the left side when they met, or to pass a slower person on the right.

10. You may not leave any horse alone on a highway in a national park.

11. It's illegal to paint your door purple in Kanata, Ontario.

ANSWERS are on page 126.

ACKNOWLEDGMENTS

One of the great things about writing a book like this is "meeting," by e-mail, letter, telephone and fax, a lot of wonderful people across the country. In spite of their own busy schedules, a lot of people found time to look up a few laws or bylaws for me. Some people sent me truckloads of laughable laws and hints about where to find others! For their generosity and big contributions to my book I would like to thank Grace Maggi, my research associate, assistant and friend; Denis Allard, office clerk, Archives Division, City Clerk Office, City of Montreal; David Bain, Librarian, Toronto Public Library; Nancy DeJager, Technical Services Librarian, Alberta Legislature Library; Larry Donaldson, Communications and Information, Kanata; Gianna Einarson, Supervisor Information Services, Office of the City Clerk, Edmonton; Marianne Fedori, President, Historical Society of Alberta; John Gervais, Manager of Communications and Information, Kanata; Ursula B. Goeres, City Solicitor, Winnipeg; Donna Henault, Bylaw Services Coordinator, Edmonton; Ed Hicks, Counsel and Informatics Coordinator, Legislative Services Branch, Department of Justice; Peter James, Regional Coordinator, Bylaw Enforcement, Halifax Regional Municipality; Donald Mitton, Supervisor, Toronto Animal Services; Helen Miller, Archivist, City of St. John's Archives, Newfoundland; Camille Morin, lawyer, Chicoutimi; Bruce Noble, City Solicitor, Fredericton, New Brunswick; Sandra Perry, Legislature Librarian, Alberta Legislature Library; Paul Waldie of *The Globe and Mail*; David Wyn Roberts, Bureau Chief, Winnipeg office of *The Globe and Mail*; Harry M. Sanders, historical consultant; Michael Vince, Manager, East District and John Walsh, Supervisor of Bylaw Enforcement, Municipal Standards, Toronto Urban Planning and Development Services.

For some choice gems and hints I thank Harry W. Arthurs, Professor of Law, York University, Toronto; John Bayly, lawyer, Northwest Territories; Sandra Black, writer, *High Park Quarterly*;

Patricia C. Clahane, Senior Solicitor, Nova Scotia Department of Justice; Margaret Crook, The Friends of the National Archives of Canada; Alix Dostal, Assistant to Rick Bartolucci, MPP for Sudbury; Allan Fineblit, Chief Executive Officer, The Law Society of Manitoba; Roy Harris, Broadcast Materials Librarian, CBC; Valerie Holder, Dean's Office, York University; Samuel Inch, NBCC Miramichi Library; M. Drew Jackson, Continuing Legal Education Society of British Columbia; Catherine Laurier, policy consultant; Linda Lovell, Secretary to the City Clerk, Windsor; Leanne MacMillan, Pink, Breen, Larkin, Halifax; Pauline Marshall, Fort Qu'Appelle, Saskatchewan; Lynn Nash, Councillor, Campbell River, British Columbia; Georgina Philips, Secretary to the Dean, University of Toronto Faculty of Law; Peter Ringrose, Executive Director, Law Society of Prince Edward Island; Lori Scott, Corporate Services Clerk, City of Quesnel, British Columbia; Lorne M. Sossin, Professor of Law, York University, Toronto; Christine Stewart, Executive Assistant, Town Manager's Office, Town of Edson, Alberta; John Tagak, Municipal Bylaw Enforcement Officer, Iqaluit, Nunavut; Wayne Tallon, St. Stephen, New Brunswick; Jeannie Wiltshire, Oshawa, Ontario; Ted Tjaden, Librarian, Bora Laskin Law Library, University of Toronto; Debbie Warrack, City Clerk's Office, City Hall, Saskatoon; staff at Montague Town Hall, P.E.I.; City Clerk's Service, City of Oshawa; John Corbett; Avery Burdett; Nathalie Ouellet; Cary Weitzman. Scores of other people listened and suggested avenues of research.

Finally I would like to express my appreciation to Sandy Bogart Johnston, Senior Editor at Scholastic Canada, who suggested the project and was a patient and tireless supporter during the compressed research and writing schedule.

Do you know of a funny Canadian law that isn't included in this book? Please send it along to the author at <bspencer@idirect.com> for possible inclusion in a second book of crazy Canadian laws.

ANSWERS

All the laws are true, except for 2, 6 and 11. Here's why:

2. Not true unless your pet rat was born wild, or weighs more than 1500 grams. Pet rats have to come from "self-sustaining captive populations." Huge pet rats are out in Toronto.

6. Not true. Livery stables could be licensed until 1996 in East York, even though this was a part of Toronto not far from downtown.

11. Not true. In some new, planned communities in Kanata, purple doors were not allowed at first. The company that built the houses filed an agreement with the city to use certain colours, and purple was not among them. Later home owners could do what they liked, though.

The publisher wishes to thank:
  Nigel Napier-Andrew for laws from THIS IS THE LAW? Doubleday Canada, 1976: 34 (bottom), 57 (top), 58 (top,middle), 60 (top), 77 (top), 81 (top), 85 (top, bottom), 91 (bottom), 100 (bottom).
  Andy Powell for laws from www.dumblaws.com: 9 (top), 29 (middle, bottom), 70 (bottom).
  Doug's Funnies collection in Funny Laws at www.stupidlaws.com for: 15 (bottom), 60 (middle).